202558

STORY:
KERRI O'HERN AND GINI HOLLAND

ILLUSTRATIONS:
ANTHONY SPAY AND ALEX CAMPBELL

WORLD ALMANAC® LIBRARY

ON THE DIXIE BELLE RIVERBOAT IN 1920, A THOUSAND PEOPLE FROM NEW ORLEANS, LOUISIANA, WAIT TO HEAR THE BAND'S NEXT SONG. A YOUNG BLACK MAN NAMED LOUIS ARMSTRONG STANDS UP TO PLAY. HIS HORN WAILS AND SINGS INTO THE NIGHT. IT IS THE ONLY SOUND HEARD. THE CROWD GOES WILD. A NEW KIND OF MUSIC IS ABOUT TO BE BORN!

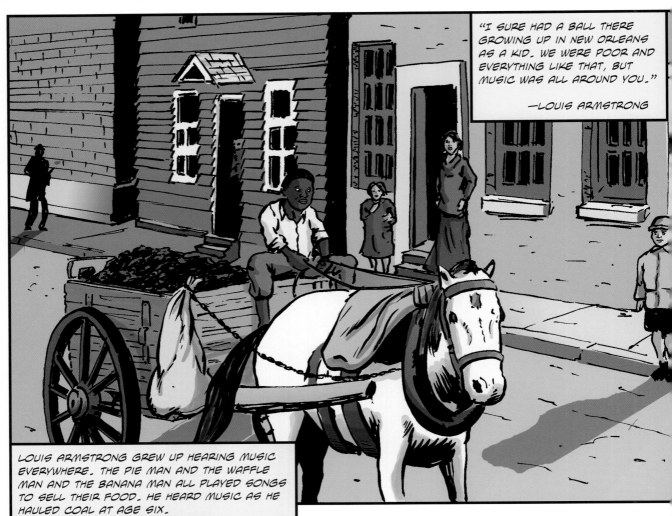

"I SURE HAD A BALL THERE GROWING UP IN NEW ORLEANS AS A KID. WE WERE POOR AND EVERYTHING LIKE THAT, BUT MUSIC WAS ALL AROUND YOU."

—LOUIS ARMSTRONG

LOUIS ARMSTRONG GREW UP HEARING MUSIC EVERYWHERE. THE PIE MAN AND THE WAFFLE MAN AND THE BANANA MAN ALL PLAYED SONGS TO SELL THEIR FOOD. HE HEARD MUSIC AS HE HAULED COAL AT AGE SIX.

HOME MADE
PIES
12¢

LOUIS AND HIS SCHOOL FRIENDS SANG ON STREET CORNERS. PEOPLE PASSING BY GAVE THEM COINS. LOUIS WOULD BRING THE MONEY HOME AND GIVE IT TO HIS MOTHER. HIS FAMILY HAD LITTLE MONEY.

KEEP THE MUSIC COMIN', FELLAS!

THEY USUALLY ATE ONLY RICE AND BEANS FOR DINNER. WHEN LOUIS BECAME RICH AND FAMOUS, HE STILL ATE THEM BECAUSE HE LIKED THEM SO MUCH. HE EVEN SIGNED HIS LETTERS "RED BEANS AND RICELY YOURS!"

NOBODY GOT HURT, BUT LOUIS WAS ARRESTED. THE COURT PLACED LOUIS IN A REFORM SCHOOL. HE WAS ELEVEN YEARS OLD WHEN HE MOVED INTO THE COLORED WAIF'S HOME FOR BOYS.

"I WAS SO SAD AND HOMESICK I WOULDN'T EAT FOR FOUR DAYS."

—LOUIS ARMSTRONG

LOUIS SOON NOTICED THAT THE SCHOOL HAD A BAND. HE HOPED THAT HE COULD JOIN AND PLAY IN PARADES AND AT PICNICS WITH THEM.

FINALLY, THE BANDLEADER TOOK A CHANCE ON LOUIS AFTER HEARING HIM SING. HE HAD HIM PLAY THE TAMBOURINE, DRUMS, AND BUGLE.

AT LONG LAST, THE LEADER LET LOUIS PLAY HIS FAVORITE INSTRUMENT, THE CORNET. LOUIS LEARNED QUICKLY. SOON HE WAS THE LEADER OF THE COLORED WAIF'S HOME BRASS BAND.

"I AM ALWAYS PROUD TO TELL THE WORLD OF THE PLACE [THAT] STARTED ME OUT AS A FIRST CLASS MUSICIAN."

—LOUIS ARMSTRONG

TWO YEARS LATER . . .

LOUIS WAS BACK HOME LIVING WITH HIS MOTHER WHEN HE STARTED WORKING TEN HOURS A DAY AT A COAL YARD . . .

AT NIGHT, HE WOULD PLAY HIS HORN AT MATRANGA'S MUSIC CLUB FOR 15 CENTS. LOUIS LOVED PLAYING ON STAGE.

JOE "KING" OLIVER WOULD COME TO MATRANGA'S TO HEAR LOUIS PLAY. SOON, THIS OUTSTANDING MUSICIAN BECAME A TEACHER AND A FRIEND TO LOUIS. HE RECEIVED HIS FIRST GOOD CORNET AS A GIFT FROM "PAPA JOE."

"HE USED TO HAVE ME TO HIS HOUSE TO EAT RED BEANS AND RICE WHICH I LOVED. HE GAVE ME LESSONS OUT OF AN EXERCISE BOOK THEN WE'D RUN DOWN LITTLE DUETS TOGETHER."

—LOUIS ARMSTRONG

IN 1918, "PAPA JOE" OLIVER TOOK A JOB WITH A BAND IN CHICAGO. HIS OLD JOB IN NEW ORLEANS NOW NEEDED A CORNET PLAYER. THE KID ORY BAND INVITED LOUIS ARMSTRONG TO FILL THE POSITION. LOUIS WAS THRILLED TO PLAY IN A BIG BAND.

ONE NIGHT, THE KID ORY BAND WAS PERFORMING ON THE BACK OF A TRUCK. THIS WAS ONE WAY NEW ORLEANS BANDS LURED CUSTOMERS TO THEIR PERFORMANCES.

FATE MARABLE'S ORCHESTRA PLAYED AT NIGHT ON THE DIXIE BELLE AS IT TRAVELED UP AND DOWN THE MISSISSIPPI RIVER.

DURING THE DAY, LOUIS LEARNED HOW TO READ MUSIC.

LOUIS STAYED WITH THIS ORCHESTRA FOR A FEW YEARS. THEN, HE DECIDED TO JOIN "PAPA JOE" OLIVER'S BAND IN CHICAGO.

THE 1920s WERE CALLED THE "ROARING TWENTIES" AND THE "JAZZ AGE." IN CHICAGO, MUSIC CLUBS WERE BOOMING. PEOPLE WAITED IN LINES TO GET INSIDE THE JAZZ MUSIC CLUBS.

"THERE WERE LOTS OF THE MUSICIANS FROM DOWNTOWN CHICAGO HURRYING FROM THEIR JOBS TO DIG US EVERY NIGHT THAT WE PLAYED AT THE LINCOLN GARDENS ON 31st STREET, NEAR THE COTTAGE GROVE AVENUE."
— LOUIS ARMSTRONG.

FOR MANY MONTHS, LOUIS PLAYED WITH OTHER PERFORMERS IN THE KING OLIVER JAZZ BAND. WHEN HE FINALLY GOT THE CHANCE TO PLAY A SOLO, HE CUT LOOSE. HIS CORONET SOARED. THE AUDIENCE LOVED HIS NEW ORLEANS JAZZ STYLE.

WORD SPREAD THAT THE NEW CORNET PLAYER IN TOWN WAS AMAZING . . .

BANDLEADERS WANTED HIM, JAZZ CLUBS WANTED HIM, AND AUDIENCES COULDN'T GET ENOUGH OF HIM! LOUIS PLAYED WITH SEVERAL DIFFERENT BANDS IN CHICAGO. HE EVEN JOINED AN ORCHESTRA THAT PLAYED ALONG WITH THE SILENT MOVIES. ARMSTRONG BEGAN TO READ AND PLAY DIFFICULT MUSIC SCORES. HE ALSO CHANGED INSTRUMENTS—HE BEGAN TO PLAY THE TRUMPET.

IN 1925, LOUIS ARMSTRONG STARTED TO RECORD MUSIC. HIS FIRST BIG HIT WAS "HEEBIE JEEBIES." FOR PART OF THE SONG, LOUIS SANG NONSENSE WORDS. FOR ONE LINE, HE SANG, "RIP-BIP-EE-DOO-DEE-DOOT, DOO." SOON, OTHERS SANG IN THIS STYLE, CALLED SCAT.

A RUMOR WENT AROUND ABOUT ARMSTRONG'S SCATTING. THE RUMOR—HE HAD DROPPED THE SHEET MUSIC WHILE RECORDING AND HAD TO MAKE UP THE WORDS. BUT LOUIS HAD BEEN SCATTING SINCE HIS DAYS SINGING ON NEW ORLEANS STREET CORNERS.

IN 1929, THE GREAT DEPRESSION BEGAN. THROUGHOUT THE 1930S, MANY PEOPLE LOST THEIR JOBS AND SOMETIMES THEIR HOMES, FARMS, AND BUSINESSES.

NEED JOB LOST EVERYTHING WILL WORK FOR

MANY HAD BARELY ENOUGH FOR THEIR BASIC NEEDS SUCH AS FOOD AND HOUSING. PEOPLE HAD LITTLE MONEY TO SPEND ON ENTERTAINMENT, SUCH AS GOING TO MUSIC CLUBS.

BECAUSE THE MUSIC CLUB BUSINESS WAS SLOW, LOUIS ARMSTRONG DECIDED TO TRAVEL AND PERFORM IN DIFFERENT PLACES.

WHILE PLAYING HIS TRUMPET IN CALIFORNIA, HE MET SOME MOVIEMAKERS. THEY LIKED HIS PERFORMANCES AND ASKED HIM TO SING IN A MOVIE.

MR. ARMSTRONG

HE MADE HIS FIRST MOVIE, EX-FLAME, DURING THIS TIME. HE ALSO RECORDED SOME MORE SONGS "I'M IN THE MARKET FOR YOU" AND "DING DONG DADDY."

BACK IN CHICAGO, SEVERAL CLUB OWNERS WANTED LOUIS TO RETURN. HIS TALENT HAD BROUGHT A LOT OF MONEY TO THEIR CLUBS.

SOME OF THESE OWNERS BELIEVED THAT ARMSTRONG SHOULD BE FORCED TO PLAY AT THEIR CLUBS. THEY CLAIMED HE HAD MADE AN AGREEMENT WITH THEM. ARMSTRONG RETURNED TO CHICAGO WITH A NEW MANAGER TO HELP HIM SETTLE THESE ISSUES.

ONE NIGHT, TWO MEN BROKE INTO ARMSTRONG'S DRESSING ROOM. THEY THREATENED HIM WITH GUNS, TRYING TO FORCE HIM TO WORK FOR THE OTHER CLUB OWNERS. AFTER THE BREAK-IN, ARMSTRONG'S MANAGER HAD POLICE OFFICERS GUARD THE DOORS BEHIND THE STAGE WHENEVER LOUIS PERFORMED.

LOUIS WANTED TO GET AWAY FROM THESE PROBLEMS IN CHICAGO. HE ALSO WANTED TO VISIT NEW ORLEANS. AFTER ALL, HE HAD NOT BEEN HOME IN NINE YEARS. IT WAS TIME TO HEAD BACK TO THE SOUTH!

OVER 2,000 PEOPLE GREETED LOUIS IN NEW ORLEANS WITH A PARADE AND MARCHING BANDS. ONLY 30 YEARS OLD, LOUIS ARMSTRONG HAD RETURNED HOME IN STYLE!

LOUIS TRAVELED WITH HIS BAND TO A FEW SOUTHERN CITIES, PLAYING FOR "WHITE-ONLY" AUDIENCES. WHILE TOURING, BAND MEMBERS WERE NOT ALLOWED INTO CERTAIN RESTAURANTS AND HOTELS. MOST NIGHTS, THEY WERE TIRED AND HUNGRY AFTER PERFORMING. THEN, THEY WOULD HAVE TO SEARCH AND SEARCH FOR A PLACE TO SLEEP THAT WOULD ACCEPT AFRICAN AMERICANS. THE RACISM THEY FACED ANNOYED AND ANGERED LOUIS AND THE BAND.

LOUIS DECIDED TO PLAY A FREE SHOW IN HIS HOMETOWN FOR AFRICAN AMERICANS. SEVERAL THOUSAND BLACK FANS SHOWED UP, BUT RACIST WHITE PEOPLE HAD BARRED THE GATES TO THE CONCERT. AT THIS TIME IN PARTS OF THE SOUTH, AFRICAN AMERICANS WHO ATTRACTED TOO MUCH ATTENTION WERE OFTEN BEATEN BY THE POLICE. SO MOST OF THESE DISAPPOINTED FANS SIMPLY WENT HOME.

AUDIENCES ALL OVER THE WORLD LOVED LOUIS ARMSTRONG. DURING THE 1930s AND 1940s, LOUIS PERFORMED IN LONDON, ENGLAND, AND OTHER EUROPEAN CITIES. SOME EUROPEAN COUNTRIES WERE MUCH MORE ACCEPTING OF BLACK PERFORMERS. ARMSTRONG LIKED PLAYING THESE CONCERTS WHERE BOTH BLACK AND WHITE PEOPLE COULD ATTEND.

LOUIS WAS A HARD-WORKING MUSICIAN. THROUGHOUT THE 1930s, 1940s, AND THE 1950s, HE PLAYED OVER THREE HUNDRED DAYS A YEAR—SOMETIMES SEVERAL TIMES IN ONE DAY. . . .

. . . AND WHILE MOST TRUMPET PLAYERS STRUGGLED TO HIT HIGH C, LOUIS COULD DO THIS 200 TIMES IN A ROW, LIGHTNING FAST.

LOUIS WAS MARRIED FOUR TIMES THROUGHOUT HIS LIFE. HE MARRIED HIS FOURTH WIFE, LUCILLE WILSON, IN 1942. LOUIS AND LUCILLE WERE TOGETHER UNTIL HE DIED IN 1971.

THEY WERE VERY HAPPY TOGETHER. LUCILLE GAVE LOUIS THE WARM HOME HE HAD NEVER KNOWN. SHE EVEN GAVE HIM HIS FIRST CHRISTMAS TREE. SHE SET IT UP IN DIFFERENT HOTEL ROOMS WHILE HE TRAVELED ON TOUR!

IN 1947, ARMSTRONG FORMED A BAND WITH BOTH WHITE AND BLACK MUSICIANS CALLED THE LOUIS ARMSTRONG ALL STARS. THE BAND BROKE SOME SOUTHERN LAWS ABOUT BLACKS AND WHITES PLAYING TOGETHER.

THIS VERY POPULAR BAND HELPED SHOW AMERICANS THAT PEOPLE OF DIFFERENT COLORS COULD WORK TOGETHER. ARMSTRONG'S HUGE POPULARITY, HIS PERSONAL CHARM, AND HIS PURE TALENT ALSO ENCOURAGED OTHER AFRICAN AMERICANS TO PURSUE THEIR DREAMS.

THE CIVIL RIGHTS MOVEMENT ALSO BACKED EQUAL RIGHTS FOR AFRICAN AMERICANS. ARMSTRONG SUPPORTED THE MOVEMENT AND KNEW HOW SLAVERY IN THE U.S. BEGAN WITH BLACKS BEING SOLD AND TAKEN FROM THEIR HOMES IN AFRICA. BECAUSE OF THESE INTERESTS, LOUIS VISITED THE CONGO IN AFRICA IN 1956. HE EVEN HAD FANS THIS FAR AWAY! FANS CARRIED HIM THROUGH THE STREETS ON A CHAIR. LOUIS ENJOYED HIS VISITS TO THE CONGO SO MUCH THAT HE RETURNED TWO MORE TIMES!

BY THE 1960s, EVERYONE KNEW LOUIS ARMSTRONG'S JAZZ. MOVIES AND TELEVISION SHOWS FEATURED THE MAN AND HIS MUSIC.

IN 1961, ARMSTRONG VISITED EGYPT WITH LUCILLE. HE PLAYED HIS TRUMPET FOR HER NEXT TO THE SPHINX AND ANCIENT PYRAMIDS.

ARMSTRONG'S JAZZ STYLE WAS ALSO A HIT ON THE POP MUSIC CHARTS. IN 1964, HIS VERSION OF "HELLO, DOLLY" KNOCKED A BEATLES' SONG FROM THE NUMBER ONE SPOT. AND IN 1968, "WHAT A WONDERFUL WORLD" BECAME A HIT ALL OVER THE WORLD.

THROUGHOUT THE 1960s, LOUIS SUFFERED FROM A SERIOUS HEART CONDITION. HE SPENT SEVERAL MONTHS IN THE HOSPITAL WITH PNEUMONIA. HIS DOCTOR ADVISED HIM TO STOP PLAYING THE TRUMPET. BUT LOUIS COULD NOT STOP PLAYING HIS MUSIC. AS LONG AS HE HAD A BREATH IN HIM . . .

HE HAD TO BLOW THAT HORN !

ARMSTRONG'S HEALTH GREW WORSE, BUT HE KEPT ON PLAYING. FOR TWO WEEKS IN 1971, LOUIS PLAYED WITH HIS ALL STARS BAND AT THE WALDORF ASTORIA HOTEL IN NEW YORK CITY. AT THE END OF THE LAST SHOW, HE COLLAPSED ON STAGE, A VICTIM OF A HEART ATTACK. A FEW WEEKS LATER, HE DIED IN HIS SLEEP.

Louis Armstrong All-Stars

MORE BOOKS TO READ

American Jazz Musicians (Collective Biographies). Stanley I. Mour (Enslow Publishers)

The Louis Armstrong You Never Knew. James Lincoln Collier (Scholastic Library)

Louis Armstrong. Trailblazers of the Modern World (series). Gini Holland
  (World Almanac Library)

The Sound That Jazz Makes. Carole Boston Weatherford (Walker Books for Young Readers)

Who Was Louis Armstrong? Yona Zeldis McDonough
  (Penguin Putnam Books for Young Readers)

WEB SITES

Jazz Greats, Louis Armstrong
pbskids.org/jazz/nowthen/louis.html

The Official Site of the Louis Armstrong House & Archives
www.satchmo.net/

Louis Armstrong
www.jazzatlincolncenter.org/educ/curriculum/modules/louisArmstrong/module.html

Louis Armstrong: A Cultural Legacy
www.npg.si.edu/exh/armstrong/index.htm

Smithsonian Jazz
www.smithsonianjazz.org/class/armstrong/la_class_1.asp

Please visit our web site at: www.worldalmanaclibrary.com
For a free color catalog describing World Almanac® Library's
list of high-quality books and multimedia programs,
call 1-800-848-2928 (USA) or 1-800-387-3178 (Canada).
World Almanac® Library's fax: (414) 332-3567.

Library of Congress Cataloging-in-Publication Data

O'Hern, Kerri.
    Louis Armstrong / Kerri O'Hern and Gini Holland.
        p. cm. — (Graphic biographies)
    Includes bibliographical references.
    ISBN 0-8368-6194-9 (lib. bdg.)
    ISBN 0-8368-6246-5 (softcover)
    1. Armstrong, Louis, 1901-1971. 2. Jazz musicians—United States—
Biography. I. Holland, Gini. II. Title. III. Series: Graphic biographies.
ML419.A75O44   2006
781.65092—dc22   2005027925

First published in 2006 by
World Almanac® Library
A Member of the WRC Media Family of Companies
330 West Olive Street, Suite 100
Milwaukee, WI 53212 USA

Copyright © 2006 by World Almanac® Library.

Produced by Design Press, a division of the
Savannah College of Art and Design
Design: Janice Shay and Maria Angela Rojas
Editing: Kerri O'Hern
Illustration: Pencils by Anthony Spay, inks by Alex Campbell, color by
    Anthony Spay
World Almanac® Library editorial direction: Mark Sachner
    and Valerie J. Weber
World Almanac® Library art direction: Tammy West

Printed in the United States of America

1 2 3 4 5 6 7 8 9 10 09 08 07 06